15325

DANVERS TOWNSHIP LIBRARY

A31300 008707

J 567.9   Hisa, Kunihiko
HIS
         The dinosaur family
         tree

DATE DUE		
FEB 1 0 1992		
FEB 2 9 1992		
MAR. 1 3 1992		
APR. 0 4 1992		
JAN. 1 4 1993		
APR 3 0 1994		
JUN. 2 4 1994		
AUG. 3 0 1994		
MAR. 0 4 1996		
AUG. 2 7 1996		

DANVERS TWP. LIBRARY
105 South West Street
Danvers, Illinois 61732
Phone: 963-4269

THE DINOSAUR FAMILY TREE

Kunihiko Hisa
Sylvia A. Johnson

DANVERS TWP. LIBRARY
105 South West Street
Danvers, Illinois 61732
Phone: 963-4269

Lerner Publications Company • Minneapolis

Rhamphorhynchus
Jurassic period

Tyrannosaurus
Cretaceous period

Triceratops
Cretaceous period

Ankylosaurus
Cretaceous period

Eudimorphodon was a pterosaur from the Triassic period. It had a wingspan of about 3 feet (1 m).

The Dinosaur Family Tree

Most people know something about dinosaurs. Tyrannosaurus, Diplodocus, Triceratops—these names are almost as well known as the names of movie stars or sports figures. But we are not so familiar with some of the other fascinating animals that shared the world of the dinosaurs.

Sea creatures like the plesiosaurs and ichthyosaurs and flying animals like the pterosaurs were all distant cousins of dinosaurs. They too lived during that ancient period of earth history known as the *Mesozoic era.* And like the dinosaurs, they disappeared from the earth at the end of the Mesozoic, about 65 million years ago.

Let's take a closer look at the animals in the dinosaur family tree to find out who they were and what kind of lives they lived. We will also try to discover what happened to these ancient animals.

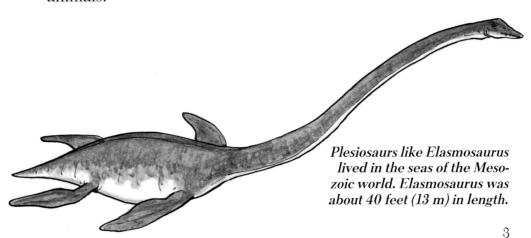

Plesiosaurs like Elasmosaurus lived in the seas of the Mesozoic world. Elasmosaurus was about 40 feet (13 m) in length.

3

Brachiosaurus

Supersaurus

Ultrasaurus

Tyrannosaurus

Compsognathus

2 m

1 m

Dinosaurs and Their Relatives

Dinosaurs came in all shapes and sizes. Some, like Brachiosaurus and its relatives (above), were giants up to 100 feet (30 m) in length. Other dinosaurs, including tiny Compsognathus, were no bigger than chickens. There were fierce meat-eating dinosaurs like Tyrannosaurus and gentle plant-eaters like Brachiosaurus and Apatosaurus. Some dinosaurs ran on two legs, while others galloped or plodded on four.

All these different kinds of dinosaurs belonged to the group of animals known as *reptiles*. Plesiosaurs, pterosaurs, and many of the other animals common in the Mesozoic era were also reptiles. Dinosaurs and their swimming and flying cousins did not look much like modern reptiles such as snakes, lizards, and turtles. Scientists also believe that some of their physical characteristics were different from those of their modern relatives. What all these ancient and modern animals share is a common chapter in the great story of *evolution*.

The first reptiles appeared at the end of the Paleozoic era, about 280 million years ago. They evolved from amphibians, animals that spent part of their lives in water and part on land. (Modern frogs and toads are surviving amphibians.) Early reptiles were all land-dwellers, but as the group evolved during the Mesozoic era, it produced animals with many different ways of life.

The illustration on the following two pages presents a simplified version of the evolution of reptiles. It also shows the way in which some reptiles developed into the animals of today.

Like dinosaurs, pterosaurs, ichthyosaurs, and mosasaurs were reptiles.

PALEOZOIC ERA

MESOZOIC

PERMIAN PERIOD

TRIASSIC PERIOD
230 to 180 million years ago

JURASSIC PERIOD
180 to 135 million years ago

THE EVOLUTION OF REPTILES

Ardeosaurus

Stegosaurus

Archaeopteryx

Seymouria

Euparkeria

Ceratosaurus

Cetiosaurus

Plateosaurus

Rhamphorhynchus

Teleosaurus

Keichousaurus

Plesiosaurus

Utatsusaurus

Ichthyosaurus

Dimetrodon

Triassochelys

Cynognathus

Morganucodon

ERA	CENOZOIC ERA
CRETACEOUS PERIOD	
135 to 65 million years ago	65 million years ago to the present

Snakes

Lizards

Mosasaurus

Mosasaurs

Tuatara

Parasaurolophus

Iguanodon

Ornithopods

Protoceratops **Triceratops**

Ceratopsians

Ornithischians
(Dinosaurs with hips like birds)

Stegosaurs

Ankylosaurus

Polacanthus

Ankylosaurs

Birds

Tyrannosaurus

Megalosaurus

Theropods

Saurischians
(Dinosaurs with hips like lizards)

Alamosaurus

Sauropods

Pteranodon

Pterosaurs

Crocodiles

Elasmosaurus

Plesiosaurs

Ichthyosaurs

Archelon

Turtles

Mammals

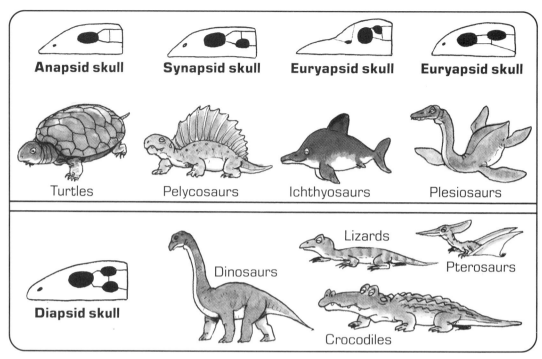

Many ancient and modern reptiles can be placed in groups based on the number of openings in their skull.

Paleontologists, scientists who study ancient life, often place all reptiles in groups based on differences in their skulls. The earliest reptiles had solid skulls with openings only for the eyes and nostrils. This skull, known as the *anapsid* type, is also found in modern turtles and tortoises. Another group of reptiles, which included animals like Dimetrodon, developed an additional pair of openings in their skulls. These *synapsid* reptiles eventually evolved into modern mammals like elephants and humans. A third type of skull with a single pair of openings is called *euryapsid*. Plesiosaurs and ichthyosaurs had this kind of skull.

During the course of their evolution, a large group of reptiles developed skulls with two pairs of openings in addition to those for the eyes and nostrils. Dinosaurs and pterosaurs had this *diapsid* skull. Crocodiles, which have changed very little since ancient times, are also diapsid reptiles, and so are modern lizards and snakes.

Looking at prehistoric reptiles in terms of their evolution and their similarities to modern reptiles is one way of studying these animals. Another way to understand dinosaurs and their relatives is by looking at the kind of environment in which they lived. Almost all dinosaurs were land animals, but some reptiles lived in the sea, while others were at home in the air. Each group had special features that suited its members to their particular environment.

Tansytropheus was an early diapsid reptile that lived during the Triassic, the first period of the Mesozoic era. About 10 feet (3 m) in length, this strange lizard-like animal may have used its long neck to catch fish from the shore.

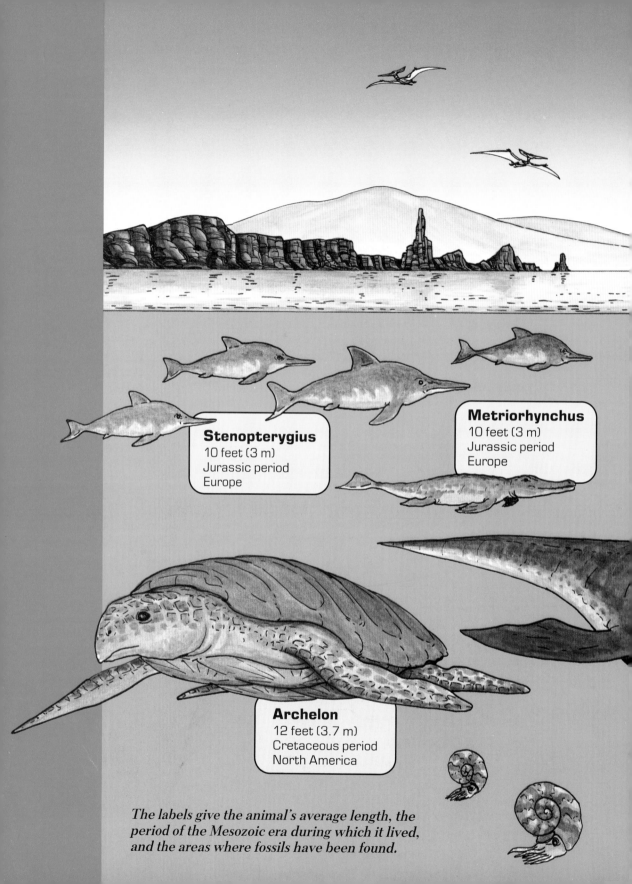

Stenopterygius
10 feet (3 m)
Jurassic period
Europe

Metriorhynchus
10 feet (3 m)
Jurassic period
Europe

Archelon
12 feet (3.7 m)
Cretaceous period
North America

The labels give the animal's average length, the period of the Mesozoic era during which it lived, and the areas where fossils have been found.

Reptiles in the Sea

Several kinds of reptiles lived in the seas of the Mesozoic world. Fish-like ichthyosaurs darted through the waters. Plesiosaurs with long necks paddled near the surface, while their short-necked relatives lurked in the depths. The seas also provided a home for marine crocodiles, lizards, and turtles.

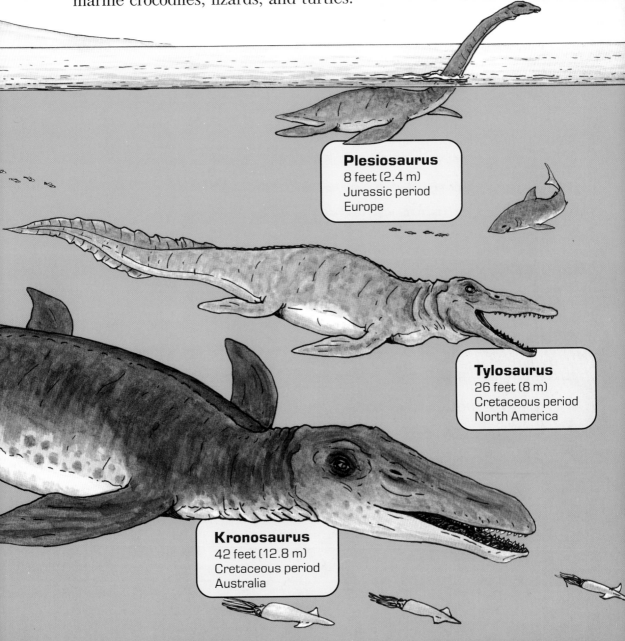

Plesiosaurus
8 feet (2.4 m)
Jurassic period
Europe

Tylosaurus
26 feet (8 m)
Cretaceous period
North America

Kronosaurus
42 feet (12.8 m)
Cretaceous period
Australia

Placodonts

Nothosaurs

Nothosaurs and placodonts were early marine reptiles, but some looked much like reptiles that lived on land. Others, such as Placochelys, the turtle-like placodont on the left, developed paddles and other features more suited to life in the water.

Return to the Sea

Like all animals with backbones, reptiles evolved from creatures that lived in the sea. The first reptiles were descended from amphibians, which had evolved from fish. All the early reptiles made their homes on land. Later, however, some members of the reptile family returned to the water, even though they continued to breathe with lungs rather than gills.

Some of the early sea-going reptiles did not look much different than their relatives that lived on land. Many placodonts and nothosaurs (above) had four legs just like land-based reptiles, although they did have webs between their toes to help in swimming. Later marine reptiles like the ichthyosaurs eventually developed flippers or fins in place of legs.

Ichthyosaurs

With their fins and streamlined, torpedo-shaped bodies, ichthyosaurs looked much like today's dolphins or sharks. They probably swam in the same manner as these modern marine animals, using their flexible tails to propel themselves rapidly through the water.

Ichthyosaurs were so well adapted to life in the water that they were unable to leave it. They could not use their fins to move around on land. These marine reptiles spent all of their lives at sea, and their babies were born in the water. Like all reptiles, ichthyosaurs produced eggs with soft shells. But ichthyosaur eggs hatched before leaving the mother's body, and the young were born alive.

Some amazing fossils found in Germany show female ichthyosaurs actually giving birth to their young. Both mothers and babies died during the process, and their bones were preserved just at the moment of birth. The drawing on the next page shows what the fossils looked like.

An ichthyosaur's streamlined body was shaped something like a submarine. As you can see in this drawing, the marine reptile's fins and tail also operated in ways similar to the working parts of a submarine.

(A) Vertical stabilization
(B) Horizontal stabilization
(C) Forward propulsion
(D) Direction control

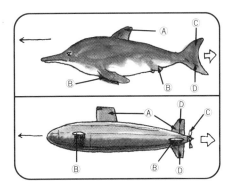

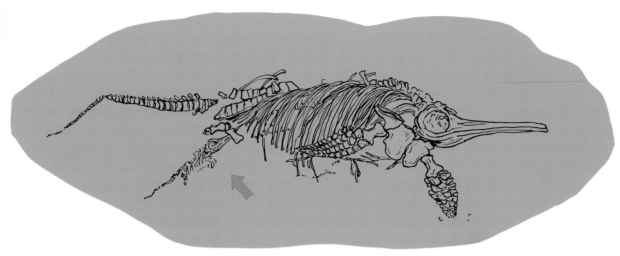

This female ichthyosaur died while giving birth to her young. The bones of both the mother and the baby were fossilized at the moment of birth.

Like all reptiles, ichthyosaurs had lungs rather than the gills of fish. As soon as baby ichthyosaurs were born, they had to come to the surface of the water in order to breathe. This scene shows how a female ichthyosaur might have helped her babies to get their first breath of air.

DANVERS TWP. LIBRARY
105 South West Street
Danvers, Illinois 61732
Phone: 963-4269

This illustration shows an ichthyosaur, Stenoptorygius, leaping out of the water as dolphins do today. Ichthyosaurs probably had many things in common with modern dolphins. There were also differences, however, including the structure of their tails. A dolphin has a horizontal tail fin, while an ichthyosaur's fin was vertical.

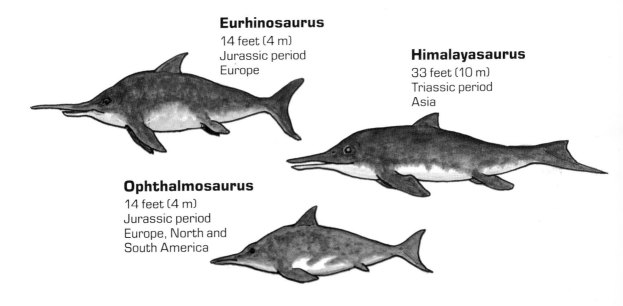

Eurhinosaurus
14 feet (4 m)
Jurassic period
Europe

Himalayasaurus
33 feet (10 m)
Triassic period
Asia

Ophthalmosaurus
14 feet (4 m)
Jurassic period
Europe, North and
South America

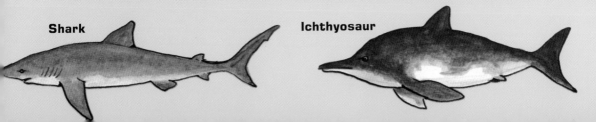

Ichthyosaurs had the same streamlined bodies as sharks, which also lived in the seas of the Mesozoic world. The animals were not related, but evolution gave them similar shapes because their ways of life were probably similar.

Shark

Ichthyosaur

Plesiosaurs may have used their flippers in a backward and forward motion to "row" themselves along (below). Another theory is that they "flew" through the water by moving their flippers up and down, as modern sea turtles do (right).

Plesiosaurs

Ichthyosaurs were around for about 100 million years, disappearing near the end of the *Cretaceous period* (the last period of the Mesozoic era). During most of this time, they shared the Mesozoic seas with another group of marine reptiles, the plesiosaurs.

Plesiosaurs did not have the streamlined bodies and flexible tails of their distant relatives the ichthyosaurs. Most paleontologists believe that they were rather slow swimmers that propelled themselves through the water with their long flippers. There are two different ways in which plesiosaurs might have used their flippers. One is by "rowing"—moving the flippers backward and forward through the water something like the oars of a rowboat.

16

Instead of rowing, plesiosaurs might have "flown" through the water by moving their flippers up and down. Modern sea turtles swim by flapping their paddle-like flippers, and they are very strong swimmers. Underwater flying might also have been the way that plesiosaurs got around.

Scientists are not sure how plesiosaurs swam, and they are also uncertain about the way they reproduced. Like the ichthyosaurs, they may have given birth to live young, but there is no fossil evidence of this. Unlike ichthyosaurs, plesiosaurs might have been able to leave the water in order to have their babies. Perhaps they reproduced like sea turtles, coming out on the shore to lay eggs. Modern marine mammals like seals also spend most of their lives at sea but come on land to bear their young. This may have been the system used by the plesiosaurs as well.

Scientists do not know whether plesiosaurs laid eggs (right) or whether their young were born alive (below).

With their paddle-like flippers, plesiosaurs may have been able to move around on land in the same way that modern seals do. This scene shows a plesiosaur, Plesiosaurus, coming out of the sea to lay its eggs on a sandy shore.

Hydrotherosaurus
45 feet (13 m)

Kronosaurus
42 feet (12.8 m)

Plesiosaurs came in two basic models. One type had a short body with a very long neck and small head. Hydrotherosaurus belonged to this group. Other plesiosaurs had long bodies with short necks and very large heads. Kronosaurus had a head bigger than that of Tyrannosaurus, one of the largest dinosaurs.

Scientists think that the long-necked plesiosaurs probably swam near the surface with their heads and necks sticking out of the water. This theory has led some people to suggest that the famous Loch Ness monster is actually a plesiosaur that survived from the Mesozoic era. Photographs taken at Loch Ness in Scotland do show something that looks like a long-necked animal in the water. But many scientists doubt that these pictures are authentic or that the "monster" really exists.

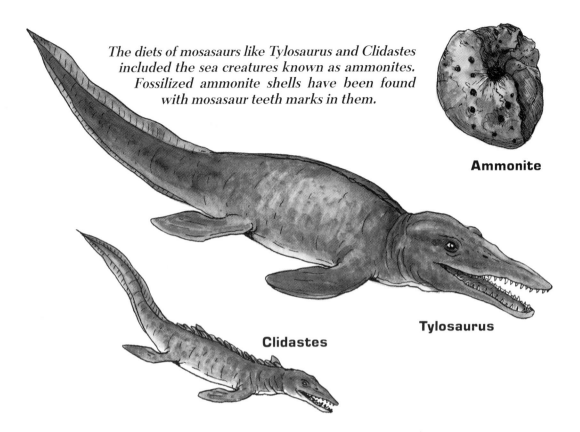

The diets of mosasaurs like Tylosaurus and Clidastes included the sea creatures known as ammonites. Fossilized ammonite shells have been found with mosasaur teeth marks in them.

Ammonite

Tylosaurus

Clidastes

Other Swimmers in the Mesozoic Seas

Plesiosaurs and ichthyosaurs were not the only marine reptiles that lived during the Mesozoic era. In the Cretaceous period, large sea-going lizards called mosasaurs became common. Mosasaurs had long, flattened tails, often with fins running along both sides. They probably used these powerful tails to push themselves through the water, steering with their flippers.

Mosasaurs had many sharp teeth, which they used to eat fish. Also included in their diets were ammonites, shell-covered animals related to modern squid. We know that mosasaurs ate these sea creatures because fossilized ammonites shells have been found with mosasaur teeth marks in them. The marine lizards had to crush the hard shells in order to get at the soft bodies inside.

Turtles and crocodiles also inhabited the seas of the Mesozoic world. Like the sea turtles of today, the giant Archelon had long flippers and a leathery covering on its back. Some of the marine crocodiles looked much like their land-dwelling cousins, with four legs and armor-covered bodies. Others, like Metriorhynchus, had flippers and a fish-like fin on their tails.

Another strange creature found in Mesozoic waters was Hesperornis, a large wingless bird. A true bird covered with feathers, Hesperornis swam by kicking with its big webbed feet. It ate the fish it caught with its small, sharp teeth.

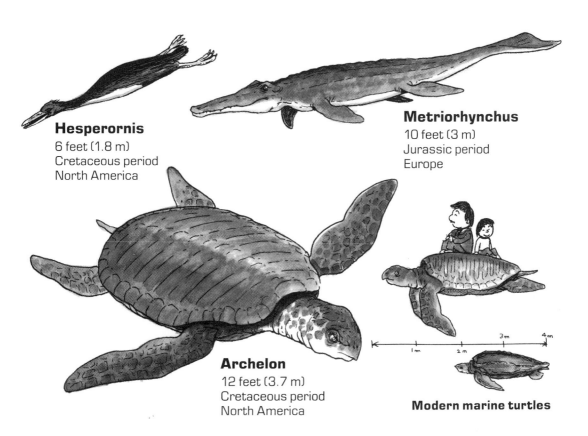

Hesperornis
6 feet (1.8 m)
Cretaceous period
North America

Metriorhynchus
10 feet (3 m)
Jurassic period
Europe

Archelon
12 feet (3.7 m)
Cretaceous period
North America

Modern marine turtles

21

Pterosaurs—the Flying Reptiles

During the Mesozoic era, reptiles not only swam in the seas but also flew through the skies. Pictured here are some of the most familiar of the pterosaurs, or flying reptiles.

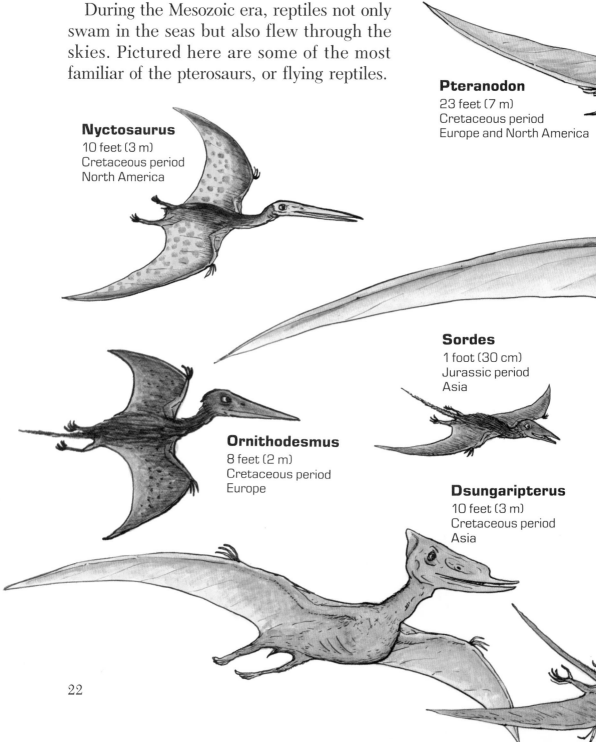

Pteranodon
23 feet (7 m)
Cretaceous period
Europe and North America

Nyctosaurus
10 feet (3 m)
Cretaceous period
North America

Sordes
1 foot (30 cm)
Jurassic period
Asia

Ornithodesmus
8 feet (2 m)
Cretaceous period
Europe

Dsungaripterus
10 feet (3 m)
Cretaceous period
Asia

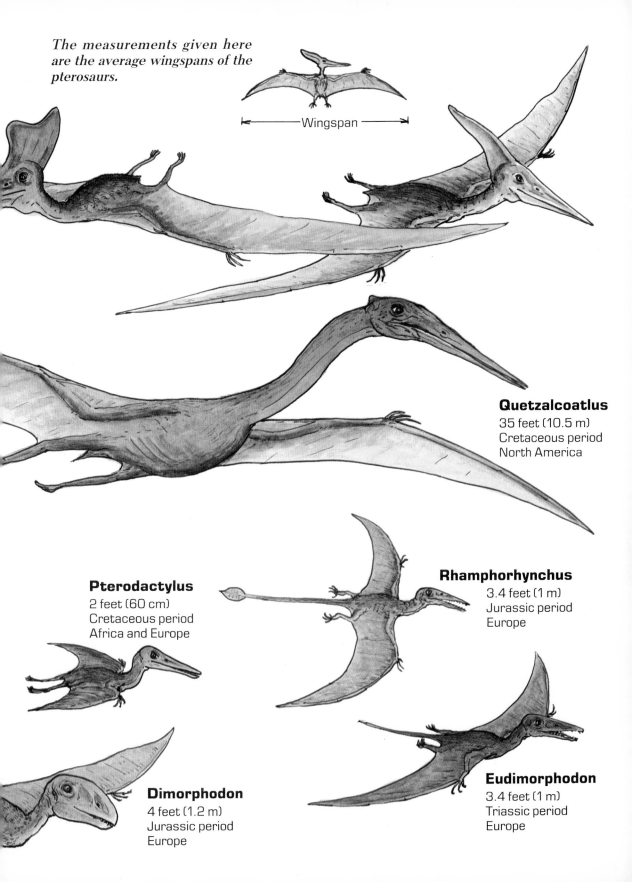

The measurements given here are the average wingspans of the pterosaurs.

Wingspan

Quetzalcoatlus
35 feet (10.5 m)
Cretaceous period
North America

Pterodactylus
2 feet (60 cm)
Cretaceous period
Africa and Europe

Rhamphorhynchus
3.4 feet (1 m)
Jurassic period
Europe

Dimorphodon
4 feet (1.2 m)
Jurassic period
Europe

Eudimorphodon
3.4 feet (1 m)
Triassic period
Europe

Some modern airborne animals fly by flapping their wings. Others glide on membranes that extend from the sides of their bodies.

There are many kinds of modern animals that take to the sky. Birds are the best-known fliers. By flapping their feather-covered wings, they can rise high into the air and travel great distances. Other expert fliers are insects and bats, which also fly by moving their wings up and down. Some animals are gliders rather than fliers. Flying squirrels, flying lemurs, and flying lizards do not have wings but instead float downward through the air on membranes that extend from the sides of their bodies.

The first reptiles to escape the gravity of earth were probably gliders. Early in the Mesozoic era, some small lizards developed body parts that enabled them to glide from a higher point to a lower one. One of the strangest of these early gliders was Longisquama, which had two rows of long, filmy scales on its back. Scientists believe that the scales acted as a kind of parachute when the little lizard leaped from tree branches.

Other early gliders like Podopteryx had flaps of skin that extended from the sides of their bodies and were attached to their four legs. It was probably from this kind of flying lizard that the great pterosaurs of the later Mesozoic developed.

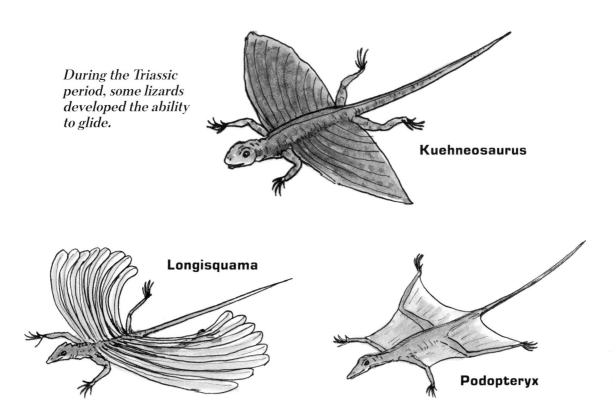

During the Triassic period, some lizards developed the ability to glide.

Kuehneosaurus

Longisquama

Podopteryx

There were many kinds of pterosaurs, with wings of different sizes and with a variety of other body features. The flying reptiles also had many different ways of life, as indicated by the fossil evidence.

Pterodactylus had fairly short wings and a long, narrow beak with small teeth in the front. It may have been an insect-eater.

This illustration shows the way in which Pterodactylus and other pterosaurs may have used the claws on their "hands" and feet to hang onto trees or climb in them.

Quetzalcoatlus was the giant among pterosaurs. This amazing animal was much larger than any modern bird, with a wingspan like that of a small airplane.

Condor
10 ft. (3 m)

Quetzalcoatlus
35-40 ft. (10-12 m)

Two-person airplane
35 ft. (10 m)

DANVERS TWP. LIBRARY
105 South West Street
Danvers, Illinois 61732
Phone: 963-4269

Quetzalcoatlus probably flew over the land and might have been a scavenger, eating the flesh of dead animals. This scene shows several of the long-necked pterosaurs feeding on the body of a large dinosaur.

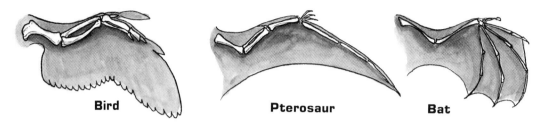

Bird   **Pterosaur**   **Bat**

The feathered wings of birds and the skin wings of pterosaurs and bats have bones similar to those in a human arm and hand. A bird's hand has only two "fingers," to which the long primary flight feathers are attached. The skin of a pterosaur's wing is stretched over a very long "little" finger, while three other finger bones stick out at the top of the wing. Like humans, a bat has five fingers. Four support the skin of the wing, while the flexible thumb is used for grasping.

How Did Pterosaurs Fly?

All scientists think that pterosaurs soared through the air, but the way in which they flew is a subject of disagreement. These ancient flying reptiles were not much like the flying animals of today. Their wings were made up not of feathers but of skin stretched over bones. Bats have wings of skin, but the bones that support them are different than those of the pterosaurs (above). Some pterosaurs, like Pteranodon and Quetzalcoatlus, had very long wings, much longer than any flying animal alive today.

Most scientists believe that the smaller pterosaurs with short, wide wings probably flew by flapping their wings as bats and birds do. Whether the large pterosaurs could fly in this way is uncertain. Many experts believe that Pteranodon may not have been able to flap its enormous wings, at least not for any length of time. They think that this pterosaur, like Quetzalcoatlus, was a glider that spread its wings and sailed along on rising currents of air.

How did Pteranodon take off for flight if it couldn't rise into the air by vigorously flapping its wings? Perhaps the pterosaur ran along the ground with its wings spread until the wind lifted it up. Some large birds, for example, albatrosses, use this method to get airborne. Or maybe Pteranodon jumped off a cliff or tree to start its flight. (The illustration below shows how this method might have worked.)

Like modern birds, Pteranodon and other pterosaurs had extremely lightweight skeletons with hollow, air-filled bones. It would have taken very little to get them off the ground. It might have been more difficult for them to return to land. Unlike birds, they had small, weak legs that wouldn't have been very useful in landing.

Pteranodon may have taken off for flight by standing on a clifftop facing in the direction of the wind (right).

The pterosaur lifts and opens its wings, allowing them to fill with air (left).

With one gentle flap of its long wings, Pteranodon rises into the air and begins its gliding flight (above).

Pteranodon had a wingspan of about 23 feet (7 m). The fossil evidence suggests that this pterosaur flew over the ocean and fed on fish.

This illustration shows a scene of Pteranodon family life, with adults bringing food to young at nesting spots along a rocky coast. Scientists know very little about Pteranodon's habits, but this is one idea about the way it lived.

Rhamphorhynchus was one of a group of pterosaurs with long bony tails. It probably fed on fish, flying low over the water and seizing them with its sharp teeth.

Dsungaripterus was a short-tailed pterosaur with a crest on its head and a beak that turned up at the end. Also a fish-eater, it may have speared its dinner with the sharp point at the end of its beak.

How Did Pterosaurs Live on Land?

Although pterosaurs were creatures of the air, they must have spent some time on land, at least when they had their young. This part of their lives is almost as much of a mystery as the way in which they flew. All pterosaurs had small, weak legs that would have made it difficult for them to walk in the way that birds do. Some scientists believe that when pterosaurs were on the ground, they hung upside down by their claws in trees or on cliff faces. This is what bats do today. Also like bats, they may have been able to move around slowly by creeping on their feet and the claws of their wings.

The long wings of some pterosaurs might also have been a problem on the ground. How did Pteranodon and Quetzalcoatlus fold their wings? Did they wrap them around their bodies like a cloak? (Some bats wrap themselves in their wings when they are hanging from a perch.) Perhaps a pterosaur's wings folded back at the finger joints so that the lower part of the wing stuck up in the air (below).

How did pterosaurs move around when they were on the ground? Did they fold their long wings to keep them from getting in the way?

"Where can I put my eggs?"

Some scientists think that pterosaurs spent most of their time on land hanging upside down from tree branches. This might have made nest building and egg laying difficult. Perhaps pterosaurs gave birth to live young. Modern bats have their babies while hanging by their feet.

The need to reproduce was one of the things that must have brought pterosaurs to land. Scientists do not know whether these animals laid eggs or gave birth to live babies, but they must have done it on land. Perhaps large numbers of pterosaurs made nests in colonies along the coasts, as many modern seabirds do. They could have laid their eggs there and left them to develop on their own. Or they might have covered the eggs to keep them warm and have taken care of the young when they hatched. Perhaps young pterosaurs were born alive, as young ichthyosaurs were. No fossil evidence has been found that can help us to answer these questions.

Archaeopteryx — Bird or Dinosaur?

During the late Jurassic period, when pterosaurs were common, another kind of winged animal was also on the scene. Unlike Pteranodon and Pterodactylus, this animal had wings covered with feathers. Scientists call it Archaeopteryx, a name that means "ancient wing." Today many experts agree that this small feathered creature was probably the first bird.

Soft materials like feathers are not usually preserved in the fossil record. But the fossils of Archaeopteryx found in Germany during the 1860s were special. They came from a rock quarry that contained limestone with a very fine grain. The rock surrounding Archaeopteryx's bones included impressions of feathers arranged just as they had been when the animal was alive.

Archaeopteryx's feathers look almost exactly like the feathers of modern birds, both in their structure and in their arrangement. The animal's bones and other body features are similar to those of a bird too. But they also have something in common with the characteristics of small, meat-eating dinosaurs like Compsognathus.

The illustrations on the opposite page compare Archaeopteryx to a modern bird, the crow. A drawing of Compsognathus is included so that you can see how similar the feathered animal is to this small, two-legged dinosaur.

34

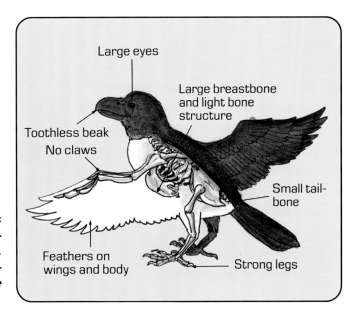

Large eyes

Large breastbone
and light bone
structure

Toothless beak
No claws

Small tail-
bone

Feathers on
wings and body

Strong legs

*Archaeopteryx (below) has
many similarities to a modern bird like the crow (right).
There are also some important differences between the
two flying animals.*

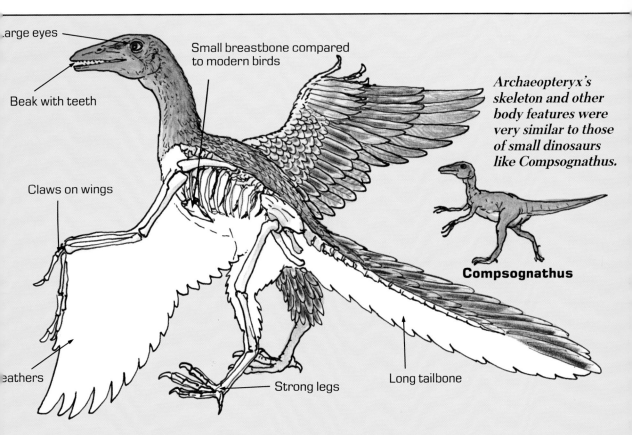

Large eyes

Small breastbone compared
to modern birds

Beak with teeth

*Archaeopteryx's
skeleton and other
body features were
very similar to those
of small dinosaurs
like Compsognathus.*

Claws on wings

Compsognathus

Feathers

Strong legs

Long tailbone

Archaeopteryx may have first developed feathers as a means of keeping warm.

Feathers on its front limbs might have been useful in scooping up insects.

Eventually, Archaeopteryx might have begun to use these feathered limbs in gliding.

Why does Archaeopteryx have some features like dinosaurs and others similar to modern birds? Paleontologists believe that this small creature was actually part dinosaur and part bird. Archaeopteryx seems to represents a final stage in the evolution that transformed certain small, quick-moving dinosaurs into modern birds.

Scientists are not sure exactly how this evolutionary change took place. Many think that during the Jurassic period, some small dinosaurs may have developed a covering of feathers instead of scales. A feather coat might have helped to keep the dinosaurs warm. Feathers on their front limbs could have been useful in scooping insects out of the air.

Being covered with feathers could have made these dinosaurs more successful in their day-to-day lives. It might have helped them to survive and produce offspring, which also had feathers. Eventually there would have been a whole group of small, dinosaur-like creatures with feathers on their bodies, limbs, and tails.

Some of these animals may have spread their feather-covered front limbs and used them in gliding down from trees. As the process of evolution continued, the limbs might have gradually developed into long, feathered wings. The small dinosaurs had become the first birds.

Paleontologists are not sure whether Archaeopteryx could actually flap its wings and fly like modern birds or whether it was only a glider. If its flight was limited to gliding down to the ground from trees, then it had to have a way to get back up again. Some scientists think that it might have climbed up by using its feet and the three clawed "fingers" of its wings.

A modern bird, the hoatzin of South America, climbs in just this way. As a chick, the bird has three clawed fingers within each wing. A young hoatzin climbs trees using these claws, as well as its feet. After it is old enough to fly, the claws drop off and the wings become fully feathered.

As a chick, the hoatzin (a South American bird) uses claws on its wings to climb in trees. Scientists think that Archaeopteryx might have climbed in the same way.

Archaeopteryx may have spent some of its time running along the ground, chasing insects and other small prey (below).

Gliding was also a part of Archae-opteryx's life (below). Scientists are not sure whether this small animal was capable of actual flight.

Among the Survivors

By the beginning of the Cretaceous period, Archaeopteryx was no longer on the scene. But many other feathered creatures flew through the skies. They were the ancestors of moderns birds, and all had evolved from Archaeopteryx or similar small reptiles.

The Cretaceous period was the last period of the Mesozoic era. When it came to an end about 65 million years ago, dinosaurs and many other reptiles disappeared from the earth. But birds survived and continued their evolution. Most scientists believe that the birds of today—from robins and owls to ostriches and penguins—are the direct descendants of the dinosaurs and their most important surviving relatives.

During the Cretaceous period, many kinds of birds evolved from Archaeopteryx and its relatives. Some were the ancestors of familiar modern species like owls and cormorants. Others, like Hesperornis and Ichthyornis, were early "toothed" birds that have no modern relatives.

Owl

Hesperornis

Ichthyornis

Cormorant

Individual dinosaurs died from many causes, including sickness and natural disasters. But the extinction at the end of the Cretaceous period was different from these individual deaths.

What Happened to the Dinosaurs?

Everyone knows that dinosaurs and other prehistoric reptiles became extinct at the end of the Cretaceous period. But what exactly does this mean? No animal or group of animals lives forever. How is this disappearance different from the fate of all living things?

During the 140 million years that they were on the earth, dinosaurs died every day. Accidents and natural disasters killed some. Others died of illness or old age or from attacks by predators. Even though these individual animals died, others like them continued to be born and to live on earth. Their group, or species, did not become extinct.

Some species of dinosaurs and other reptiles did disappear completely before the end of the Cretaceous period. Stegosaurs were common during the Jurassic period, but by the second half of the Cretaceous, they were no longer around. The flying reptile Rhamphorhynchus and its relatives became extinct by the beginning of the Cretaceous. These animals left no descendants; no others of their kind ever lived on earth again.

What happened at the end of the Cretaceous period was different from the deaths of many individual animals or even the disappearance of a few groups. At this time, all groups of dinosaurs and most other reptiles became extinct. In fact, more than half of **all** living things—animals and plants—were wiped out of existence. This extinction did not take place overnight, but it did happen and it was final.

GONE FOREVER

Paleontologists tell us that extinction is not a rare occurrence. During the millions of years of earth history, many species of animals— for example, mammoths—have disappeared completely.

Mammoth

Moa

In recent times, the dodo, the moa, and the passenger pigeon have all become extinct.

Passenger pigeon

Dodo

The fossil evidence shows that there have also been several mass extinctions. One of the greatest took place at the end of the Permian period, about 248 million years ago, when half of all animal life on earth was wiped out. The disappearance of dinosaurs and their relatives was part of another important mass extinction.

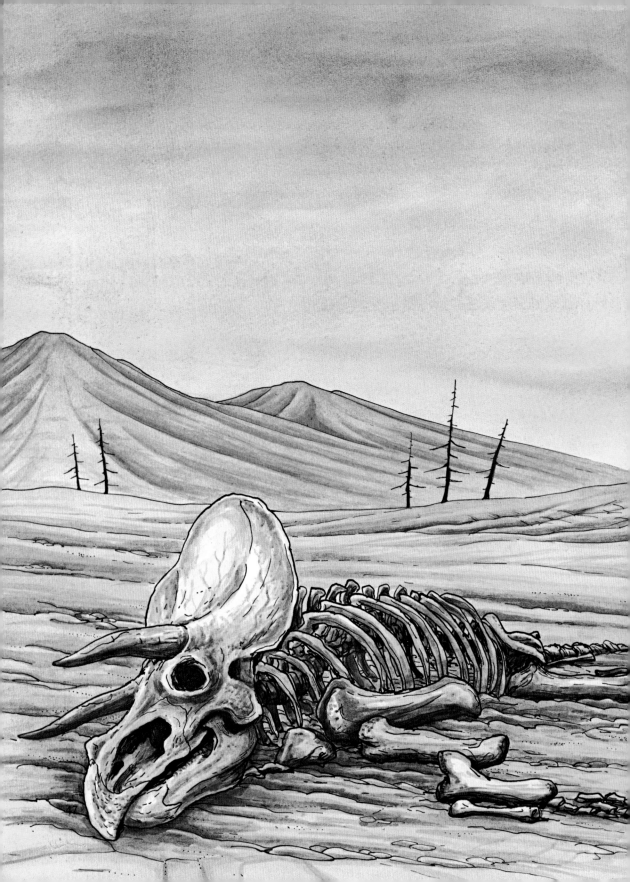

Triceratops was one of the most common kinds of dinosaurs during the late Cretaceous period. Large herds of these great horned animals wandered throughout western North America. After the end of the Cretaceous period, Triceratops and its relatives were gone. What was it that killed these dinosaurs and so many other living things?

DANVERS TWP. LIBRARY
105 South West Street
Danvers, Illinois 61732
Phone: 963-4269

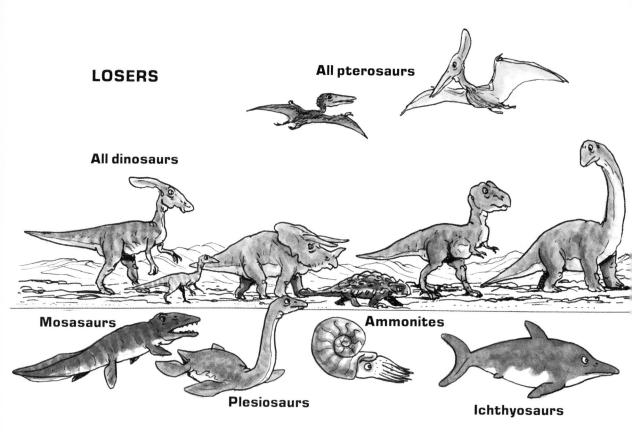

LOSERS

All pterosaurs

All dinosaurs

Mosasaurs

Plesiosaurs

Ammonites

Ichthyosaurs

Losers and Winners

In thinking about what happened at the end of the Cretaceous period, it is important to remember one thing. Not all animals or even all reptiles became extinct. There were some survivors, including our own distant ancestors.

First, let's look at the list of losers in the battle against extinction. It is a long list, and it includes many kinds of creatures. All dinosaurs became extinct, along with their flying relatives, the pterosaurs. In the sea, the plesiosaurs and mosasaurs were wiped out. Not many ichthyosaurs were still around by this time, but the disaster at the end of the Cretaceous got rid of any remaining members of this group of marine reptiles. Many other sea creatures, including the spiral-shelled ammonites, also disappeared.

The list of winners is shorter but contains some interesting and important members. A few reptiles survived, including the ancestors of today's crocodiles, lizards, turtles, and snakes. Birds, those feathered descendants of the dinosaurs, continued to fly through the sky. And creeping around on the ground were some small, cat-sized animals that would eventually develop into the mammals of today.

The fact that there were both winners and losers is one of the things that makes the extinction at the end of the Cretaceous period so complicated. Scientists have many different theories about what happened, and so far, none seems to be completely satisfactory. But most experts believe that some theories work better than others in explaining this mysterious event.

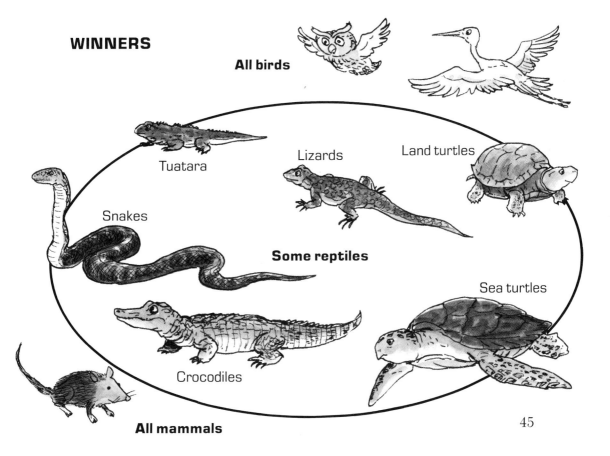

WINNERS

All birds

Tuatara

Lizards

Land turtles

Snakes

Some reptiles

Sea turtles

Crocodiles

All mammals

45

A Changing Climate

Many scientists believe that the extinction at the end of Cretaceous period was caused by worldwide changes in climate. These changes might have taken place over thousands of years, but their total effect was enough to alter the environments in which many animals lived. Groups of animals that could not adjust to the new conditions or find other places to live eventually became extinct.

What could have caused such significant changes in the earth's climate? Some scientists think that the changes may have been related to movements in the *plates* that make up the surface of the earth. Such movements have always been a part of the earth's history. But at the end of the Cretaceous period, they may have been so widespread that they resulted in devastating changes.

Shifting Plates

Geologists, scientists who study the earth, tell us that the earth's outer layer is broken up into a number of large, rigid plates. These plates slide slowly on the soft material that lies beneath them. As they move, they carry with them the continents and the ocean floors.

Over the millions of years of earth history, the continents have changed position several times. At the beginning of the Mesozoic era, when the first dinosaurs appeared, all the earth's land was joined in one supercontinent. During the next 100 million years, this great land mass broke up and drifted apart, propelled by the movement of the plates.

A shift in the positions of continents is only one result of movements of the earth's plates. When the edges of two plates grind

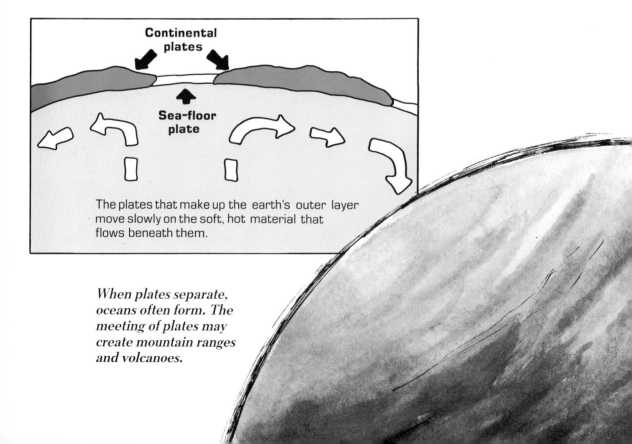

The plates that make up the earth's outer layer move slowly on the soft, hot material that flows beneath them.

When plates separate, oceans often form. The meeting of plates may create mountain ranges and volcanoes.

together, great mountain ranges like the Himalayas may be created. Sometimes the meeting of plates produces conditions that cause earthquakes and volcanoes. In areas where plates are separating from each other, oceans may form.

Scientists believe that the end of the Cretaceous period may have been a time of great plate activity. The drifting continents were approaching their present positions, although India had not yet joined the rest of Asia. Some of the earth's oceans were widening, while others were shrinking or disappearing. Volcanoes were erupting in many parts of the world, throwing large amounts of ash and other material into the air. All these things could have affected the earth's climate, although scientists do not agree on exactly what the effects might have been.

During the period of plate activity at the end of the Cretaceous period, volcanic eruptions may have produced great clouds of ash and dust.

The volcanic ash and dust in the air might have cut down the amount of sunlight reaching the earth. Colder temperatures would have resulted and perhaps long periods of cold rains.

Without adequate light from the sun, plants would have suffered. As plant life changed or died out in certain areas, plant-eating animals might not have been able to get enough to eat. Because the continents were separated from each other, the animals could not easily move to other areas to find food, as they had in the past. When groups of plant-eaters began to disappear, the meat-eaters that depended on them for food were also threatened.

Climate changes at the end of the Cretaceous period could also have affected the earth's oceans and their inhabitants. The drop in temperature may have killed many of the tiny animals and plants on which larger sea creatures depended for food.

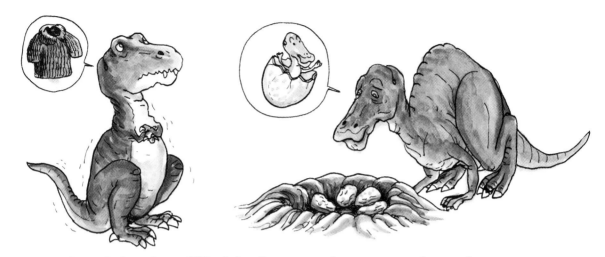

It might have been difficult for dinosaurs to keep warm and to produce young in a cold climate.

A Different World

Faced with colder temperatures and lack of food, the animals of the late Cretaceous would have responded in different ways. Small animals covered with fur or feathers had a much better chance of surviving the cold than large animals with no coverings on their naked skins. These small creatures would also need less food to stay alive than large animals.

During this period of environmental change, animals like birds and mammals also had an advantage in the way that they produced their young. Birds sit on their eggs to keep them warm until they hatch. Mammals keep their young inside their bodies until they are developed and, after birth, feed them with milk.

Dinosaurs and most other reptiles did not sit on their eggs, and they could not produce food to feed their babies. These animals would have found it difficult to raise young during a period of cold and scarce food. Without offspring, they were on their way to extinction.

Reproduction would have been easier for birds and mammals.

Comparing reptiles to birds and mammals might help to explain why dinosaurs became extinct and the small furred and feathered creatures survived. What it doesn't explain is why reptiles like snakes, lizards, and crocodiles were also among the survivors. Some scientists have come up with a solution to this puzzle. They think that these reptiles survived because they were *ectotherms*, or cold-blooded animals. Dinosaurs and other large reptiles like the pterosaurs became extinct because, like birds and mammals, they were *endotherms* (warm-blooded animals).

Endotherms have internal heating systems that have to be fueled by food. But small endotherms covered with feathers or fur need less fuel than large animals without such coverings.

Ectotherms can survive on very little food because they have no internal heating system to maintain. When temperatures drop, their body temperatures fall too, and all their body functions slow down. In this state of inactivity (which is something like hibernation), the animals might be able to survive until living conditions improve.

The animals and plants that disappeared at the end of the Cretaceous period were gone forever. During the next period of earth history, other living things gradually took their places. In this new world, reptiles did not play a very large role. Instead of dominating the land, sea, and sky as they had during the Cretaceous period, they were limited to special kinds of environments. Birds took over the skies, while fish and other creatures multiplied in the seas. On land, the small mammals came out of their hiding places to assume an important role in this changed world.

Other Ideas about the Extinction of the Dinosaurs

Many scientists believe that the dinosaurs were killed by gradual climate changes caused by volcanic eruptions and other events resulting from movements of the earth's plates. But there are other scientists who have different ideas on the subject. Let's take a quick look at some of them.

Death from Outer Space An increasing number of scientists believe that the dinosaurs and their relatives died because of a violent catastrophe, which caused great devastation all over the world. They suspect that, near the end of the Cretaceous period, the earth was struck by a giant asteroid hurtling through space.

The impact of the asteroid caused a tremendous explosion that sent up great clouds of dust. Dust spread over the earth and blocked light from the sun for months or even years. Without sunlight, plants on land and in the oceans died, and the climate turned cold. Many animals could not adapt to these conditions and became extinct.

An asteroid striking the earth might seem rather improbable, but there is some evidence to support the theory. In samples of rock deposited during the late Cretaceous period, scientists have found large amounts of a metal called iridium. Rocks from many parts of the world contain this material, which is rare on earth but common in asteriods and meteorites. An asteroid collision with the earth that produced enormous amounts of dust would explain the existence of this iridium layer.

DANVERS TWP. LIBRARY
105 South West Street
Danvers, Illinois 61732
963-4269

Some scientists think that dinosaurs might have been killed by radiation coming from the explosion of a giant star.

Another theory claims that dinosaurs died out because the small, clever mammals of the late Cretaceous period ate all their eggs.

Poison produced by newly evolved flowering plants has also been blamed for the extinction of dinosaurs. Plant-eaters could have eaten the deadly plants and passed the poison on to meat-eaters.

Their Own Fault Some of the older ideas about extinction suggest that the dinosaurs themselves were to blame. They were too large and too stupid to compete with the small, clever mammals that had appeared in the Cretaceous world. Another idea was that the dinosaurs, pterosaurs, and other reptiles had been around for such a long time and had evolved into such strange forms that they were unable to adapt to new environments.

Theories that blame dinosaurs for their own extinction are no longer accepted by most scientists. The most popular current ideas are those that see some general change in living conditions as the cause. The change may have taken place suddenly or slowly. It may have been a result of volcanoes erupting on earth or asteroids coming from space. Whatever its cause, it brought to an end the existence of all the dinosaurs and many of their relatives.

The Age of Birds and Mammals

The extinction of the dinosaurs marked the end of one era in earth history and the beginning of a new one. During the *Cenozoic era*, mammals and birds would play a very important role.

Birds had begun their development during the Cretaceous period. In the early part of the Cenozoic era, many different kinds of birds appeared. Most were fliers, but some spent all their time on the ground, like today's ostriches. One flightless bird was Diatryma (below), which lived about 55 million years ago.

Diatryma lived in Europe and North America during the early part of the Cenozoic era. This giant bird was about 7 feet (2 m) tall. Equipped with a hooked beak and strong claws, it may have been a predator and meat-eater.

Baluchitherium was an early rhinoceros from Asia. The largest land mammal ever known, it was about 28 feet (8 m) long and weighed around 33 tons.

Mammals too evolved rapidly during the first part of the Cenozoic era. The furry little creatures of the Cretaceous eventually developed into many different kinds of animals, including giants like Baluchitherium (above).

Mammals were like dinosaurs in the variety of forms they took and the different environments in which they lived. Also like the dinosaurs, they came to dominate their world. The Age of Mammals began 65 million years ago, and it is still going on today.

Animals in the Dinosaur Family Tree

Archaeopteryx (ar-kee-OP-ter-iks)—the first known bird, which probably evolved from small dinosaurs during the Jurassic period

Archelon (ARK-ih-lohn)—a large sea turtle from the late Cretaceous period in North America

Baluchitherium (ba-loo-chih-THER-ee-uhm)—the largest land mammal known, a relative of the modern rhinoceros. From the early Cenozoic era in Asia

Clidastes (klie-DAS-teez)—a mosasaur, or marine lizard, that lived during the late Cretaceous period in North America

Diatryma (die-uh-TRY-muh)—a giant flightless bird from the early Cenozoic era. Fossils found in Europe and North America

Dimorphodon (die-MOR-fuh-don)—a pterosaur, or flying reptile, from the early Jurassic period in Europe

Dsungaripterus (suhn-gahr-IP-tuhr-us)—a pterosaur from the Cretaceous period in Asia with a bony crest on its head

Elasmosaurus (ee-laz-moh-SAWR-uhs)—a long-necked plesiosaur from the late Cretaceous period in Asia and North America

Eudimorphodon (you-dih-MOR-fuh-don)—a pterosaur related to Rhamphorhynchus, from the late Triassic period in Europe

Eurhinosaurus (you-rhine-uh-SAWR-uhs)—an ichthyosaur with a very long upper jaw, from the early Jurassic period in Europe

Hesperornis (hes-per-OR-nis)—a large wingless bird with teeth that inhabited North American seas during the late Cretaceous period

Himalayasaurus (him-ih-lay-uh-SAWR-uhs)—an ichthyosaur from the Triassic period in Asia

Hydrotherosaurus (hy-dro-ther-uh-SAWR-uhs)—a long-necked plesiosaur from the Cretaceous period in North America

Ichthyornis (ik-thee-OR-nis)—a toothed sea bird from the late Cretaceous period in North America

Kronosaurus (kron-uh-SAWR-uhs)—a plesiosaur with a short neck and large head, from the Cretaceous period in Australia

Kuehneosaurus (kyou-nee-oh-SAWR-uhs)—a gliding lizard from the Triassic period in Europe

Longisquama (long-jih-SKWAM-uh)—a lizard-like animal from the Triassic period in Asia with long scales on its back

Metriorhynchus (met-ree-oh-RINK-uhs)—a marine crocodile with flippers and a fish-like tail. From the Jurassic period in Europe

Nyctosaurus (nik-toh-SAWR-uhs)—a pterosaur from the Cretaceous period in North America

Ophthalmosaurus (ohf-thal-moh-SAWR-uhs)—an ichthyosaur with very large eyes, from the Jurassic period in Europe and North and South America

Ornithodesmus (or-nith-uh-DEZ-muhs)—a pterosaur from the Cretaceous period in Europe

Placochelys (plak-uh-KEE-lis)—a placodont (an early marine reptile) with a turtle-like body and flippers. From the Triassic period in Europe

Plesiosaurus (plee-zee-oh-SAWR-uhs)—an early plesiosaur from the Jurassic period in Europe

Podopteryx (poh-DAHP-tuhr-riks)—a gliding lizard from the Triassic period that may have been an ancestor of pterosaurs

Pteranodon (teh-RAN-uh-don)—a very large pterosaur from the Cretaceous period in Europe and North America

Pterodactylus (tehr-uh-DAK-tih-luhs)—a pterosaur from the late Jurassic period in Africa and Europe

Quetzalcoatlus (ket-zahl-ko-ATL-uhs)—the largest of the pterosaurs, from the late Cretaceous period in North America

Rhamphorhynchus (ram-fuh-RINK-uhs)—a pterosaur with a long tail, from the Jurassic period in Europe and Africa

Sordes (SOR-deez)—a small pterosaur from the Jurassic period in Asia. Some fossils seem to show that Sordes's body was covered with fur.

Stenopterygius (sten-op-tuh-RIDG-ee-us)—an ichthyosaur from the Jurassic period in Europe.

Tansytropheus (tan-zee-TROHF-ee-us)—a lizard-like animal with a very long neck, from the Triassic period in Asia and Europe

Tylosaurus (tie-luh-SAWR-uhs)—a mosasaur from the Cretaceous period in Europe and North America

Glossary

anapsid (uh-NAP-sihd)—having a solid skull with openings only for the eyes and nostrils. The earliest reptiles and modern turtles have this kind of skull.

Cretaceous (creh-TAY-shus) period—the third and final part of the Mesozoic era. At the end of this period (about 65 million years ago), dinosaurs and many other kinds of animals became extinct.

diapsid (die-AP-sihd)—having a skull with two pairs of openings in addition to those for the eyes and nostrils. Dinosaurs, pterosaurs, crocodiles, lizards, and snakes are diapsid reptiles.

ectotherms (EK-toh-therms)—animals whose body temperatures are controlled by the temperature of the environment. Insects and modern reptiles are ectotherms, but scientist are not sure whether dinosaurs and other prehistoric reptiles had this kind of temperature-control system.

endotherms (EN-doh-therms)—animals whose body temperatures are controlled from within. Birds and mammals are endotherms, and many scientists believe that pterosaurs and dinosaurs may also have belonged to this group.

euryapsid (yur-ee-AP-sihd)—having a kind of skull with a single pair of openings in addition to those for the eyes and nostrils. Plesiosaurs and ichthyosaurs were euryapsid reptiles.

evolution—the gradual process of change by which animals and plants develop from earlier forms of life. Evolutionary change usually takes place in response to changes in the environment.

Jurassic (juhr-ASS-ik) period—the second part of the Mesozoic era, from about 180 to 135 million years ago

Mesozoic (mehz-uh-ZOH-ik) era—the 160-million-year period of earth history during which dinosaurs, pterosaurs, and other prehistoric reptiles lived

paleontologists (pay-lee-ohn-TAHL-uh-jists)—scientists who study prehistoric life

plates—the large, rigid segments that make up the earth's outer layer. These plates, which are about 30 to 90 miles (48 to 144 km) thick, move slowly on the soft, hot material that lies beneath them.

reptiles—animals with backbones that have dry, scaly skin and breathe with lungs. Modern reptiles such as snakes, lizards, and crocodiles are all ectotherms, but some dinosaurs and other early reptiles may have been endotherms.

synapsid (sin-AP-sihd)—having a kind of skull with one pair of openings in addition to those for the eyes and nostrils. Some early reptiles like the pelycosaurs had synapsid skulls. Modern mammals evolved from this line of reptiles.

Index

Kunihiko Hisa created the Discovering Dinosaur books because he wanted to introduce young people to the real dinosaurs, animals that lived successfully on earth for more than 100 million years. In preparing the books, Mr. Hisa visited museums and excavations and studied the most recent discoveries of paleontologists around the world. His lively illustrations and informative texts are based on this research and on his own ideas about what dinosaurs were like and how they lived.

Sylvia A. Johnson is a writer and editor of science books for young people. In adapting the Discovering Dinosaur books for English-speaking readers, she made use not only of her scientific background but also of her experience in working with dinosaur fossils. As a volunteer in a museum laboratory, Ms. Johnson cleaned and repaired the bones of dinosaurs like Camarasaurus and Diplodocus. This first-hand experience helped her to appreciate just how "real" dinosaurs were.

This edition first published 1990 by Lerner Publications Company.
Original edition published 1983 by Akane Shobo Company, Ltd., under the title KYORYU WA NAZE HORONDA KA?
Text and illustrations copyright © 1983 by Kunihiko Hisa.
Additional text for this edition copyright © 1990 by Lerner Publications Company.
English translation rights arranged with Akane Shobo Company, Ltd., through Japan Foreign-Rights Centre.
Translation of original text by Wesley M. Jacobsen.

All rights to this edition reserved by Lerner Publications Company.
No part of this book may be reproduced, stored in a retrieval system, or transmitted in any form or by any means, electronic, mechanical, photocopying, recording, or otherwise, without the prior written permission of the publisher, except for the inclusion of brief quotations in an acknowledged review.

Library of Congress Cataloging-in-Publication Data

Hisa, Kunihiko. 1944-
  [Kyōryū wa naze horonda ka? English]
  The dinosaur family tree / Kunihiko Hisa and Sylvia A. Johnson.
     p.   cm.
  Translation of: Kyōryū wa naze horonda ka?
  Summary: Discusses different kinds of dinosaurs, their possible fate, and other animals to which they may have been related.
  ISBN: 0-8225-2203-9
  1. Dinosaurs—Juvenile literature. [1. Dinosaurs.] I. Johnson, Sylvia A. II. Title
QE862.D5H59213   1990
567.9′1—dc20
                                                    90-13215
                                                        CIP
                                                        AC

Manufactured in the United States of America
1 2 3 4 5 6 7 8 9 10 99 98 97 96 95 94 93 92 91 90